With Love to:

....

From:

....

The Gift of SOLITUDE
©Scandinavia Publishing House
Drejervej 15,3 DK-Copenhagen NV
Denmark
Tel. +45-3531 0330
www.scanpublishing.dk
info@scanpublishing.dk

Scripture Selection by Carol A. Kauffman
Designed by Ben Alex

ISBN 978-87-7247-322-2

THE GIFT OF
SOLITUDE

QUOTES FROM THE HOLY BIBLE

scandinavia

My people
will live in safety,
quietly at home.
They will be at rest.

ISAIAH 32:18 (NLT)

In quietness
and confidence
is your strength.

ISAIAH 30:15B (NLT)

"My soul is
crushed with grief
to the point of death.
Stay here and keep
watch with me."

MATTHEW 26:38 (NLT)

"Be silent,
and know that I am God!
I will be honored
by every nation.
I will be honored
throughout the world."

PSALM 46:10 (NLT)

Restore us, O Lord,
and bring us back
to you again!
Give us back the joys
we once had!

LAMENTATIONS 5:21 (NLT)

Return,

O my soul,

to your rest;

for the Lord

has dealt bountifully

with you.

PSALM 116:7 (NRSV)

The beloved
of the Lord rests in safety
- the High God surrounds him
all day long - the beloved rests
between his shoulders.

DEUTERONOMY 33:12 (NRSV)

I, yes I,
am the one
who comforts
you.

ISAIAH 51:12A (NLT)

Remember
your promise to me;
it is my only
hope.

PSALM 119:49 (NLT)

Now let your
unfailing love
comfort me,
just as you
promised me,
your servant.

PSALM 119:76 (NLT)

I am
my beloved's
and my beloved
is mine.

SONG OF SOLOMON 6:3 (NRSV)

You will keep
in perfect peace
all who trust in you,
whose thoughts
are fixed on you!

ISAIAH 26:3 (NLT)

All night long
I search for you;
in the morning I earnestly
seek for God.

ISAIAH 26:9 (NLT)

Be still
in the presence
of the Lord,
and wait patiently
for him to act.

PSALM 37:7A (NLT)

The Lord himself
watches over you!
The Lord stands beside you
as your protective shade.

Psalm 121:5 (NLT)

He makes me
lie down in green pastures,
he leads me beside quiet waters,
he restores my soul.

PSALM 23:2-3A (NIV)

The Lord keeps
watch over you
as you come and go,
both now and forever.

PSALM 121:8 (NLT)

I have stilled
and quieted my soul;
like a weaned child
with its mother,
like a weaned child is
my soul within me.

PSALM 131:2 (NIV)

You can be sure of this:
The Lord set apart
the godly for himself.
The Lord will answer
when I call to him.

PSALM 4:3 (NLT)

The one thing
I ask of the Lord
– the thing I seek the most –
is to live in the house of the Lord
all the days of my life.

PSALM 27:4A (NLT)

How lovely is
your dwelling place,
O Lord of Heaven's Armies.
I long, yes, I faint with longing
to enter the courts
of the Lord.

PSALM 84:1-2a (NLT)

Since the first day
you began to pray
for understanding and
to humble yourself
before your God,
your request has been
heard in heaven.

DANIEL 10:12B (NLT)

His peace
will guard your hearts
and minds as you live
in Christ Jesus.

PHILIPIANS 4:7B (NLT)

I lie awake
thinking of you,
meditating on you
through the night.

PSALM 63:6 (NLT)

Because you
are my helper,
I sing for joy
in the shadow
of your wings.

PSALM 63:7 (NLT)

I cling to you;
your strong right hand
holds me securely.

PSALM 63:8 (NLT)

O God,
you are my God;
I earnestly search
for you.

PSALM 63:1A (NLT)

Let all that I am
wait quietly before God,
for my hope is in him.

PSALM 62:5 (NLT)

Let me live forever
in your sanctuary,
safe beneath the shelter
of your wings!

PSALM 61:4 (NLT)

The Lord is close
to all who call on him,
yes, to all who call
on him in truth.

PSALM 145:18 (NLT)

Surely goodness
and lovingkindness
will follow me all the days
of my life, and I will
dwell in the house of
the Lord forever.

PSALM 23:6 (NASB)

Those
who look
to the Lord
will have every
good thing.

PSALM 34:10B (NCV)

"Come to me,
all who labor
and are heavy laden,
and I will give you rest."

MATTHEW 11:28 (RSV)

There remains,
then, a Sabbath-rest
for the people
of God.

HEBREWS 4:9 (NIV)

He said,
My presence
shall go with thee,
and I will give
thee rest.

EXODUS 33:14 (ASV)

My people will live
in a peaceful habitation,
and in secure dwellings
and in undisturbed
resting places.

ISAIAH 32:18 (NASB)

"Accept my teachings
and learn from me,
because I am gentle
and humble in spirit,
and you will find rest
for your lives."

MATTHEW 11:29 (NCV)

You hide them
in the shelter of
your presence,
safe from those who
conspire against them.
You shelter them
in your presence,
far from accusing tongues.

PSALM 31:20 (NLT)

Cast your burden
upon the Lord
and He will sustain you;
He will never allow
the righteous
to be shaken.

PSALM 55:22 (NASB)

Do not rejoice
over me, O my enemy;
when I fall, I shall rise;
when I sit in darkness,
the Lord will be
a light to me.

MICAH 7:8 (NRSV)

God is our protection
and our strength.
He always helps us
in times of trouble.

PSALM 46:1 (NCV)

The Lord is good,
a refuge in times of trouble.
He cares for those
who trust in him.

NAHUM 1:7 (NIV)

I urge you,
as aliens and strangers
in the world, to abstain
from sinful desires.

1 PETER 2:11 (NIV)

An angel from heaven
appeared to him and
strengthened him.
And being in anguish,
he prayed more earnestly,
and his sweat was like drops
of blood falling on
the ground.

LUKE 22:43-44 (NIV)

I will not
leave you
comfortless:
I will come
to you.

JOHN 14:18 (KJV)

He who dwells
in the shelter
of the Most High
will rest in the shadow
of the Almighty.

PSALM 91:1 (NIV)

Take delight in the Lord,
and he will give you
the desires of your heart.

PSALM 37:4 (NRSV)

Whoever finds me
finds life and receives
favor from the Lord.

Proverbs 8:35 (NIV)

You are my hiding place;
you protect me from trouble.
You surround me with
songs of victory.

PSALM 32:7 (NLT)

This God is our God
for ever and ever;
he will be our guide
even to the end.

"I will restore
you to health
and I will heal you
of your wounds,"
declares the Lord.

Jeremiah 30:17 (NASB)

Be of good courage,
and he shall strengthen
your heart, all ye
that hope in the Lord.

PSALM 31:24 (KJV)

The eternal God
is thy refuge,
and underneath
are the everlasting arms.

Deuteronomy 33:27a (KJV)

Even if
my father and mother
abandon me, the Lord
will hold me close.

PSALM 27:10 (NLT)

He leads me
beside still waters;
He restores my soul.

PSALM 23:2B-3A (NASB)